HEADS UP!

A LOOK INSIDE SKULLS

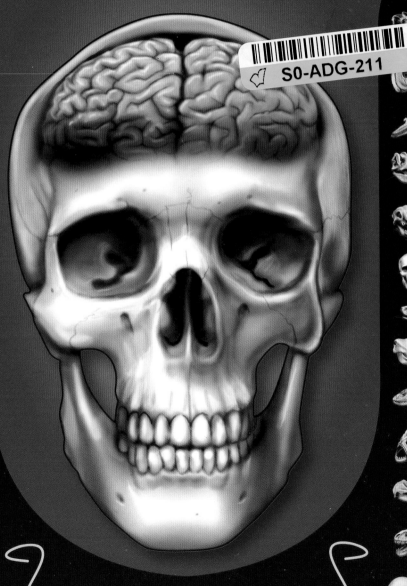

S0-ADG-211

BY **PAUL BECK**

Skulls
Copyright © 2006 becker&mayer!
Published by Tangerine Press, an imprint of
Scholastic Inc.
557 Broadway; New York, NY 10012
All rights reserved.

Scholastic and Tangerine Press and associated logos
are trademarks of Scholastic Inc.

No part of this book may be reproduced, stored in
a retrieval system, or transmitted in any form or by
any means, electronic, mechanical, photocopying,
recording, or otherwise, without the prior permission
of Tangerine Press.

Produced by becker&mayer!, LLC.
11010 Northup Way
Bellevue, WA 98004
www.beckermayer.com

If you have any questions or comments about this
product, send e-mail to infobm@beckermayer.com

Written by Paul Beck
Art direction and design by Scott Westgard
Skull illustrations and
assembly illustrations by Ryan Hobson
Additional illustrations by Joshua Beach
Edited by Don Roff
Product development by Todd Rider
Production management by Katie Stephens
Fact checking and image research by Zena Chew

Printed, manufactured, and assembled in China.

0-439-87692-3

10 9 8 7 6 5 4 3 2 1

05382

What holds your brain in,
gives your eyes a place to look out of,
and keeps your hat from falling down
onto your neck?

IT'S YOUR SKULL!

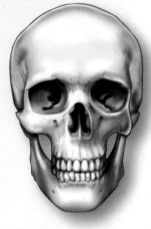

TABLE OF CONTENTS

SKULLJOBS

Skulls come in different shapes and sizes—from gigantic whale skulls to tiny minnow skulls. But they all do the same job. They protect brains. They hold and protect the sense organs like the eyes, ears, and nose. And they provide a framework and anchor for the muscles and tissues of the face, head, and neck.

HUMAN   PIRANHA   EAGLE   DOLPHIN

KOMODO DRAGON   WILD BOAR   SABER-TOOTH   T. REX

DRY BONES

You may think that bones like skulls are dry and brittle, but they're really alive. Living bones have blood vessels and nerves running through them. The outside layer of a bone is hard and solid, called compact bone. Inside that layer is spongy bone. It's called spongy because it's full of holes, but it's not soft. It's strong but light. The holes in the spongy bone are filled with red bone marrow, a jelly-like material that makes red blood cells.

BLOOD VESSELS

COMPACT BONE

SPONGY BONE

OLD **BONES**

Skulls have been around a long, long time. The first skulls belonged to fish that lived during the Cambrian Period, over 500 million years ago. These were the first vertebrates, or animals with backbones.

SKULL-ETON?

The hagfish is an animal whose skull is its only skeleton. These slimy scavengers live on the muddy ocean floor. Hagfish have a primitive skull made of cartilage, the same flexible material that is in the stiff parts of your ears. Hagfish have a spinal cord, but no backbone and no other bones. A hagfish is so flexible that it can tie itself in a knot.

BRAINS

No matter what kind of animal a skull belongs to, there's a brain inside. Brains are made of neurons (NURE-ons), or nerve cells. These long cells carry electrical signals and connect to each other in complicated networks. All animals' brains are divided into parts that do different jobs. Brains take care of controlling the body and its organs, sensing the outside world, solving problems, learning, and remembering.

BRAIN SIZES

Some brains are bigger than others, but that doesn't always mean they're brainier. Bigger animals have bigger brains because the animals themselves are bigger. A better way for guessing an animal's intelligence is to compare the brain size to the animal's body size. Also, look to see how complicated the brain's structure and connections are.

HUMAN

Humans belong to the order (large group of related animals) called primates. The primates also include apes, monkeys, and other animals such as lemurs. The shape of a human skull gives a clue about one of humans' most important features: our big brains.

A human skull isn't all one piece. It's made up of 22 separate bones in two main groups: the cranium and the face bones.

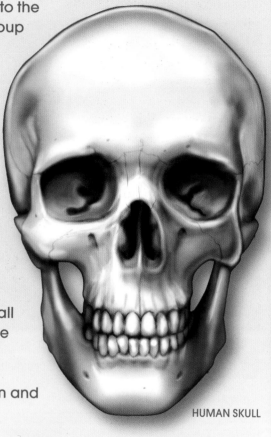

HUMAN SKULL

FACE BONES ||||||||||||||||||||||||||||||||||||||||||||||||||||||||||||||||||||||

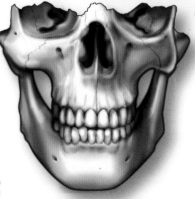

Part of the skull is made up of bones of the face. There are 14 of them. These bones form the eye sockets, cheekbones, jaws, and the roof of the mouth. The jawbones hold the hardest and toughest part of the human body: the teeth. The lower jaw, or mandible, is the only bone in the skull that can move freely.

THE CRANIUM

The cranium (CRAY-nee-um) is the round part of the skull that protects the brain. Another name for the cranium is the braincase. It is made of eight flat bones like curved plates.

The bones of the cranium are connected to each other by joints called sutures (SOO-chers). The sutures look like squiggly lines. In kids' skulls these joints are made mostly of flexible cartilage. As you get older, more and more of the cartilage turns into bone. But the cranial sutures don't completely harden until a person is 40 or 50 years old.

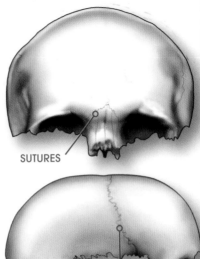

SUTURES

SUTURES

THE BRAIN

In an adult human, the brain that fits inside the skull is a little bigger than two fists put together. It weighs about three pounds (1.4kg).

The outer layer of the brain is called the cerebral cortex (suh-REE-bruhl CORE-tex). It takes care of many of the complicated things we do, including thinking, processing information from the senses, solving problems, talking, and understanding language.

The cerebral cortex is folded into bumps and grooves so that its gigantic surface area can fit inside the skull. If you could unfold a human cerebral cortex, it would be about the size of a full-sized sheet of newspaper.

CEREBRAL CORTEX

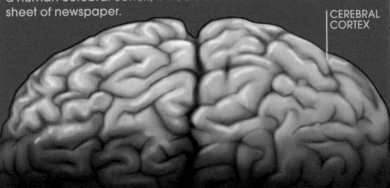

DOLPHIN

A dolphin's skull shows some of the ways these mammals are adapted for living and hunting in the ocean. A dolphin's brain is bigger than a human brain. Like a human's, the dolphin's cerebral cortex has a large surface area with many folds and bumps. However, much more of a dolphin's brain is used for the sense of hearing. That's because a dolphin's main way of getting information is through sonar, which is using sound waves they emit to find objects under water.

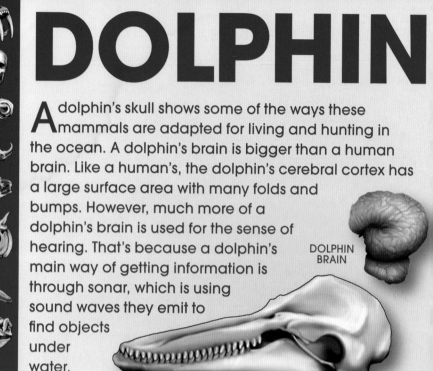

DOLPHIN BRAIN

DOLPHIN SKULL

A NOSE ON TOP

The top of the dolphin's skull has a double hole. This is the nasal opening, like the one in your skull behind your nose. Dolphins are mammals, which means they have lungs and breathe air. A dolphin breathes through an opening in the top of its head called the blowhole. On the surface of the dolphin's skin, the blowhole is a single opening. Beneath the skin the opening divides into two air passages, like your nostrils.

NO CHOKING

Unlike yours, a dolphin's windpipe and esophagus are completely separate. Food goes into the stomach through the mouth, and air goes into the lungs through the blowhole. A dolphin can't choke on its food.

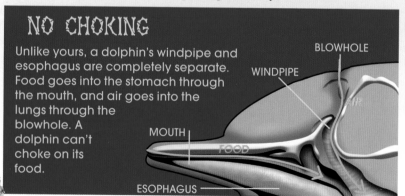

BLOWHOLE

WINDPIPE

MOUTH

FOOD

ESOPHAGUS

SEEING WITH SONAR

Humans get most of their picture of the world around them from their sense of sight. Dolphins can "see" their surroundings using echolocation (sonar) and their sense of hearing. The dolphin makes sounds in the form of clicks. The sound waves travel through the water. When the waves strike an object, such as a fish, they bounce off and echo back to the dolphin. Using information from the sonar echoes, the dolphin's brain tells it where the object is.

A dolphin's forehead has a large bulge. But there's no bulge on the skull. The bulge on the dolphin's forehead is created by a sac filled with oily, waxy fat. Because of its shape, this lump of fat is called the melon. The fat carries sound waves. The melon acts like a lens for sound waves. It focuses the dolphin's sonar clicks into a tight beam that the dolphin can aim very precisely.

A JAW TO HEAR WITH

Believe it or not, a dolphin hears with its lower jaw! Its jawbone is thin and hollow. The hollow space is filled with the same type of sound-carrying fat as the melon. The bone picks up sound vibrations, and the fat in the jaw carries the vibrations up into the skull to the dolphin's inner ear.

EAGLE

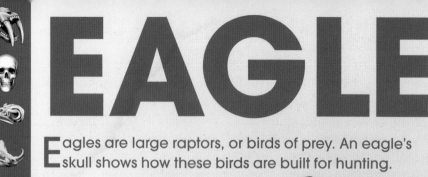

Eagles are large raptors, or birds of prey. An eagle's skull shows how these birds are built for hunting.

Birds' skulls are very light compared to the skulls of mammals and reptiles. Instead of thick, heavy bone like that of a human skull, the bones in an eagle's skull are thin and light. Most of them are made of two thin layers of bone, separated by a small space and connected by small pillars. The lower jaw is light and delicate. Birds have no teeth, so an eagle doesn't need a big jaw for biting and chewing. Its beak tears at food, like the flesh of small rodents.

EAGLE SKULL

BEAK

The front parts of the jaws form the eagle's beak. The beak is made of bone covered with a sheath of keratin, the same material that your fingernails are made of. Like your fingernails, the keratin covering the beak keeps growing all the time. The edges of an eagle's beak are sharp. The tip is hooked and pointed, for tearing prey.

EAGLE **EYED**

One look at the eagle's skull will tell you what its most important sense is—its sight. Eagles need sharp eyes for spotting prey from high in the air. An eagle's eyes have over five times more light-sensing cells than a human's. That means the eyes are enormous. In fact, an eagle's eyes take up more space in its skull than its brain does.

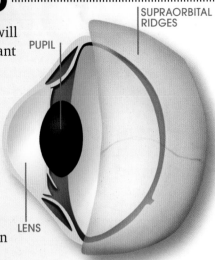

SUPRAORBITAL RIDGES

PUPIL

LENS

EAGLE EYE

A ring of thin, bony plates surrounds and protects most of the front of each eye. Above the eyes are two big shelves of bone called supraorbital (SOO-pruh-OR-bit-uhl) ridges. They protect the eyes from injury and shade them from the sun. These ridges are what give an eagle its stern look.

An eagle's eyeballs aren't round like a human's. Instead, the back of the eye is bigger and flatter. Only the very front is visible in the eagle's face. Due to the size and shape of their eyes, the eagle can't move them at all. To look in different directions, an eagle has to turn its whole head.

BIRDBRAIN

An eagle's brain would fit in a tablespoon and weighs about as much as four quarters. Bird brains don't have a folded cerebral cortex like mammal brains. But that doesn't mean they're less intelligent than other types of animals. Their brain cells are connected in a complicated network that handles information the way mammal brains do.

11

WILDBOAR

Wild boars are the ancestors of all domestic pigs. They live in Europe, Asia, and North Africa. In the 1800s, wild boars were brought to North America for hunting. They bred with domestic pigs that had gone wild, so the wild boars now living in the United States are hybrids, or mixed species.

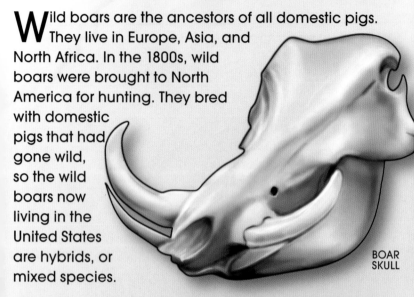

BOAR SKULL

EAT LIKE A PIG ||||||||||||||||||||||||||||||||||||||||||||||||

Wild boars are omnivores (AHM-nuh-vors), which means they eat both plants and meat. You can tell by looking at the teeth. The front teeth are sharp and pointed for biting meat, while the rear teeth (molars) are flat for chewing and grinding plants.

A wild boar's food is 90% plants. They dig for roots, bulbs, and tubers (potato-like roots) with their tough snouts. They also eat fruits and berries. The other 10% of their food can include mice, small birds, snakes, lizards, insects, and eggs. Boars also eat carrion (dead animals).

TUSKS

The tusks are the wild boar's canine teeth. Females don't grow big tusks. The male's tusks can grow to be as long as 5 inches (12.7 cm). Both the top and bottom tusks stick out of the mouth and grow upward. The upper tusks rub against the lower ones and keep them razor-sharp. Boars use their tusks for rooting in the ground for food. The males also use them for fighting.

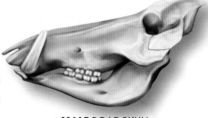

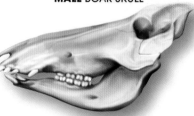

MALE BOAR SKULL

FEMALE BOAR SKULL

ALWAYS GROWING

A male wild boar's tusks start growing when it is about two years old and keep growing for the rest of its life.

BOAR **BRAIN**

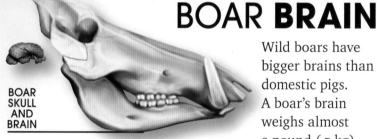

BOAR
SKULL
AND
BRAIN

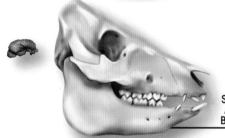

PIG
SKULL
AND
BRAIN

Wild boars have bigger brains than domestic pigs. A boar's brain weighs almost a pound (.5 kg). A pig's brain weighs a third less than that. Most domestic animals have smaller brains than their wild cousins.

SWINE SENSES

A wild boar's best sense is its sense of smell. The boar's sensitive snout can sniff out underground roots and tubers. Because the boar's eyes aren't nearly as sharp as its tusks, it relies on its excellent hearing for navigation in low light.

T. REX

Tyrannosaurus rex is the tyrant lizard king. It was one of the biggest predators to ever walk the earth. This dinosaur lived in North America between 70 and 65 million years ago. One look at a fossilized T. rex skull is all it takes to tell how this animal made its living.

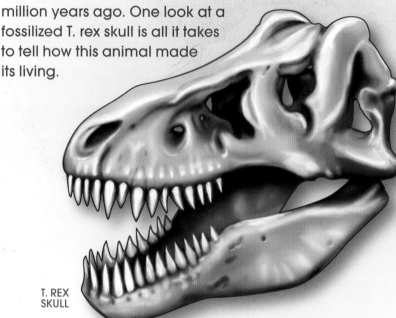

T. REX SKULL

HERE'S **LOOKING** AT YOU!

A T. rex's eye sockets were big enough to hold eyes the size of baseballs. As with many predators, the Tyrannosaurus's eyes faced forward. Forward-facing eyes give an animal depth perception, or the ability to tell how close or far away an object is. Each eye gets a slightly different view, and the brain uses that information to give the animal 3-D vision.

BIG HEAD

The biggest T. rex skull fossil ever found is more than 5 feet (1.5 m) long and 3 feet (.9 m) wide. That's about the size of a refrigerator!

BIG, **BIG BITE!** |||||||||||||||||||||||||||||||||||||||

A T. rex's jawbones were massive and heavy, with a lower jaw that could grow up to 4 feet (1.2 m) long. From the size of the area where the jaw muscles attached, scientists know that this dinosaur had a lot of muscle in its bite. A T. rex could chomp down with more than 2,000 pounds (907 kg) of pressure, enough to crush the bones of the dinosaurs that it ate.

A Tyrannosaurus's teeth were built for crushing and tearing. The biting part of the tooth was shaped like a long, curved cone. The front and back edges had lots of sharp points. The biggest T. rex teeth fossils are more than a foot (.3 m) long, but less than half of the tooth actually stuck out from the gums. The other half was anchored deep in the jawbone.

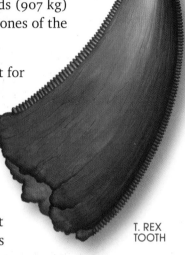

T. REX TOOTH

NO BRUSHING OR FLOSSING NEEDED

A Tyrannosaurus rex grew new teeth throughout its life. If a tooth broke or fell out, there was always a new one to take its place. This dinosaur's mouth was always filled with teeth of different sizes, some growing and some fully grown.

DINO **BRAIN** |||||||||||||||||||||||||||||||||||||||||||||||||||||||

A T. rex's brain was shaped more like a cylinder than a sphere. As with many predators, the brain areas for the sense of sight were large. The olfactory part of the brain was also very big, which meant that Tyrannosaurus had a good sense of smell.

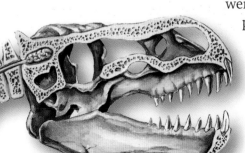

T. REX SKULL AND BRAIN

SABERTOOTH

Different types of saber-toothed cats lived at different times during the history of mammals. The biggest and most well-known is the Smilodon. This fearsome-looking predator became extinct at the end of the last ice age, around 10,000 years ago. Many fossils of this saber-toothed cat have been found in the Rancho La Brea tar pits in California. Other now-extinct animals that lived at the same time include mammoths, mastodons, and giant sloths. Humans were also spreading across the world at that time.

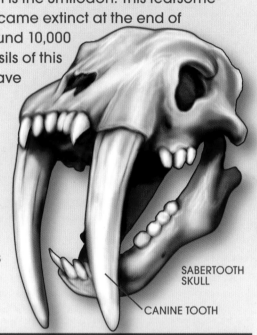

SABERTOOTH
SKULL

CANINE TOOTH

WHERE'S THE TIGER?

Smilodon is sometimes called the saber-toothed tiger, but it wasn't actually related to tigers. It was a bit shorter than a modern lion but almost twice as heavy. It also had a stubby tail, like a bobcat's.

This saber-toothed cat's coat probably wasn't striped like a tiger's, either. A tiger's stripes help it stay hidden in the forested areas where it lives. Smilodon lived in the grasslands, so it's more likely this cat had a coat like the lions of today.

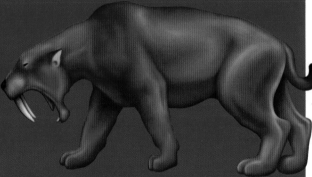

16

TEETH OF MYSTERY |||||||||||||||||||||||||||||

A Smilodon skull is a little longer than a football, but each of the gigantic canine teeth could be up to 7 inches (17.8 cm) long. It's a sure bet these teeth were for hunting, but scientists aren't sure exactly how the cat used them. The sabertooth may have used them to grab and hold onto prey, but this cat's jaws didn't have a strong bite for an animal of its size. It's more likely that Smilodon used its canine teeth as weapons for slashing or stabbing.

ALL TOGETHER NOW

Scientists have determined from saber-tooth fossil samples that due to disease and injury, not all cats were able to hunt. For survival, the non-hunting cats must have lived in a group and relied on other cats that hunted. Today, lions are the only cats that live in groups, called a pride. All others, like tigers and leopards, are solitary hunters.

SABERTOOTH BRAIN |||||||||||||||||||||||||||||

The sabertooth had a fairly small brain for an animal of its size. Compared to a modern lion, the braincase is smaller and flatter.

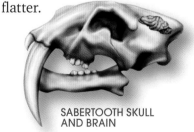

SABERTOOTH SKULL
AND BRAIN

LION SKULL
AND BRAIN

PIRANHA

Piranhas live in South American rivers. These fish have a reputation for being vicious and dangerous. But piranhas only become the bone-stripping killers of legend when they're not getting enough to eat. There are several different species of piranhas. Most grow to be 6 to 10 inches (15 to 25 cm) long, but some species are larger. The biggest is almost 2 feet (.6 m) long!

The piranha skull is made of many small bones. Its skull has a lot of open space. Both of these things help to keep the fish's skeleton light. A heavy skeleton would slow the fish down in the water.

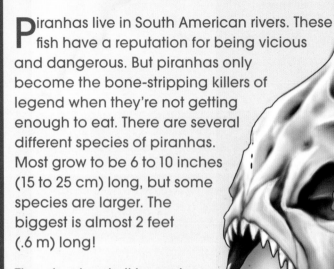

PIRANHA SKULL

SIGHT AND SMELL

Like most fish, a piranha has its eyes on the sides of its head. The eyes bulge out from the face, giving the fish a wide view all around its body. A piranha can even see some of what is going on behind it.

A piranha has two small holes in the front of its face, just where you would expect its nose to be. In fact, those are the fish's nostrils, called nares. Since fish don't breathe, the nares are not connected to its throat. Instead, they just open into a space lined with smell-sensing nerves.

NARES

RAZOR **MOUTH**

One look at a piranha's jaws suggests how they got their killer reputation. They're lined with razor-sharp, triangular teeth. When a piranha loses a tooth, another one grows in to take its place. The lower jaw is powerful and sticks out farther than the upper one. The teeth fit together like the jaws of a trap.

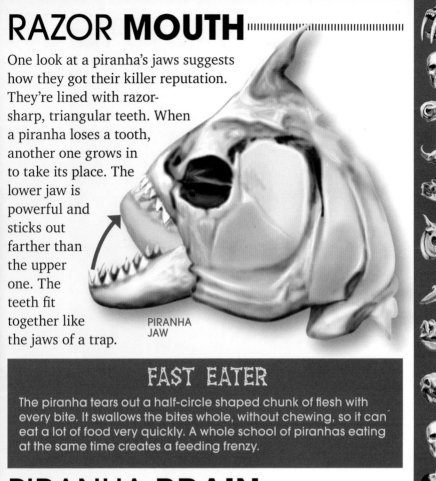

PIRANHA JAW

FAST EATER

The piranha tears out a half-circle shaped chunk of flesh with every bite. It swallows the bites whole, without chewing, so it can eat a lot of food very quickly. A whole school of piranhas eating at the same time creates a feeding frenzy.

PIRANHA **BRAIN**

A piranha's brain is small. Still, like the brains of all the animals in this book, the fish's brain is divided into three sections. At the front, the forebrain handles just the fish's sense of smell. The midbrain takes care of learning, muscle reactions, and the sense of sight. The hindbrain handles movement and balance.

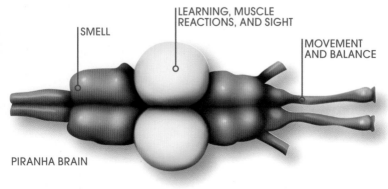

SMELL

LEARNING, MUSCLE REACTIONS, AND SIGHT

MOVEMENT AND BALANCE

PIRANHA BRAIN

KOMODO DRAGON

Komodo dragons, also known as Komodo monitors, are the largest lizards in the world. They live in Indonesia. They can grow to be as long as 10 feet (3m) and weigh up to 300 pounds (136 kg). Komodo dragons are carnivores, or meat-eaters. They hunt live animals like deer, goats, and wild boars. They are also scavengers, eating dead animals that they find.

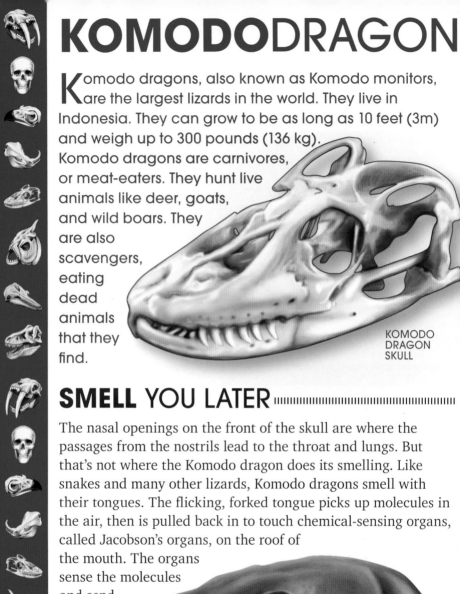

KOMODO DRAGON SKULL

SMELL YOU LATER

The nasal openings on the front of the skull are where the passages from the nostrils lead to the throat and lungs. But that's not where the Komodo dragon does its smelling. Like snakes and many other lizards, Komodo dragons smell with their tongues. The flicking, forked tongue picks up molecules in the air, then is pulled back in to touch chemical-sensing organs, called Jacobson's organs, on the roof of the mouth. The organs sense the molecules and send messages to the brain.

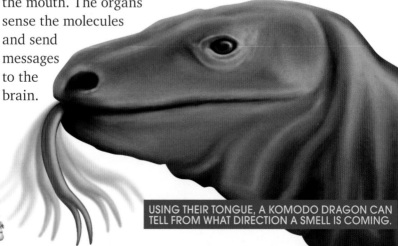

USING THEIR TONGUE, A KOMODO DRAGON CAN TELL FROM WHAT DIRECTION A SMELL IS COMING.

DRAGON **JAWS** |||||||||||||||||||||||||||||||||||||||||||||||

The Komodo dragon's main weapon is its teeth. When hunting, it attacks with jaws and claws, tearing its prey to pieces. The lower jaw opens very wide, allowing the lizard to take gigantic bites. It swallows the big chunks of meat with its powerful jaw and throat muscles.

A Komodo dragon can eat as much as 80% of its own weight in one sitting. It can also throw it all back up again if it needs to lighten its load to run away.

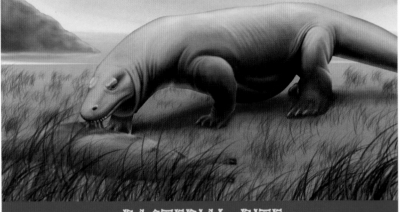

BACTERIAL BITE

A Komodo dragon's teeth have lots of sharp points. When bits of meat from a meal become stuck in the teeth, the meat rots in the lizard's mouth, growing bacteria. In fact, the Komodo dragon's saliva is chock full of infection-causing bacteria. When the Komodo dragon bites its prey, the bacteria causes the wounds to become infected. Even if the animal escapes, it eventually dies of blood poisoning, and the patient Komodo dragon can find the carcass and eat.

DRAGON **BRAIN** |||||||||||||||||||||||||||||||||||||||||||||||

A Komodo dragon's brain is about the size of your thumb. Reptile brains are long rather than round in shape. Similar to the piranha, the Komodo dragon's brain is divided into three sections: forebrain, midbrain, and hindbrain. The forebrain handles the sense of smell. The midbrain takes care of vision, learning, and voluntary (not automatic) actions. The hindbrain handles the other senses, the internal organs, and automatic actions, like balance and coordination. In the animal world, reptillian brains are considered the most simple.

21

EXTREMESKULLS

BIG SKULL ||||||||||||||||||||||||||||||||||||||||||||||||||||||||||||||||||||||||||||

As you might expect, the biggest skull belongs to the biggest animal, the blue whale. This ocean giant's skull can be as long as a school mid-bus and weigh as much as an elephant.

BLUE WHALE SKULL

MID-BUS

20 FEET (6.07 M)

SMALL SKULL ||||||||||||

The skull of the tiny bumblebee bat is only about ½ inch (11 mm) long, or the size of two pencil erasers. The whole bat weighs less than a dime and is the world's smallest mammal.

BUMBLEBEE BAT SKULL

WRONG SKULL

From 1934 to 1979, the fossil skeleton of the dinosaur known at the time as Brontosaurus was on display at the Carnegie Museum of Natural History...with the wrong head! The skull on the skeleton belonged to another dinosaur, Camarasaurus. It was only after 45 years that the wrong skull was replaced with the correct one. It was the skull belonging to a dinosaur discovered earlier, called Apatosaurus. Since Brontosaurus and Apatosaurus turned out to be the same, the dinosaur now goes by the name of the first-discovered fossil: Apatosaurus.

WIDE SKULL

The skull of the Irish elk isn't as amazing as the antlers attached to it. This extinct, moose-like animal lived in Europe during the last ice age, around the same time that Smilodon lived in North America. Its gigantic antlers had a span of up to 12 feet (3.7 m). The Irish elk was the largest deer that ever lived.

IRISH ELK
SKULL AND
ANTLERS

THICK SKULL

The domed skull of the dinosaur Pachycephalosaurus was 10 inches (25 cm) thick on top. For a long time, people thought these dinos used their skulls in head-butting contests. But the bone turned out to be porous. If smacked together, the skulls would break. Instead, Pachycephalosaurus may have used its skull to drive away rivals or predators by ramming them in the sides.

OLD SKULL

The oldest skull of a hominid (human-like ancestor) found so far is between six and seven million years old. It was found in Chad.

The oldest skull of Homo sapiens, a modern-day human, was found in Ethiopia. It is 160,000 years old.

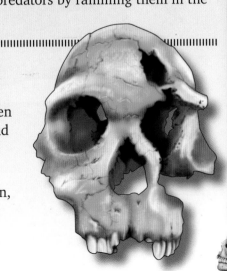

EXTREMEBRAINS

HEAVY BRAIN ||||||||||||||||||||||||||||||||||||||||||||||||||||||||||||||||

An elephant's brain weighs about 13 pounds (6 kg), 4⅓ times more than a human brain. But remember—an elephant weighs about 60 times more than a human.

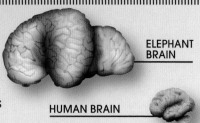

ELEPHANT BRAIN

HUMAN BRAIN

EXTRA BRAIN ||||||||||||||||||||||||||||||||||||||||||||||||||||||||||||||||

Did you ever wish you had an extra brain to bring to school when you have a test? For a long time people thought giant dinosaurs like Apatosaurus had a second brain at the base of their tails. Now scientists believe the "extra brain" was really an enlarged part of the spinal cord, like a relay station for messages to the back end of the animal. But this enlarged part of the spinal cord was bigger than the animal's real brain!

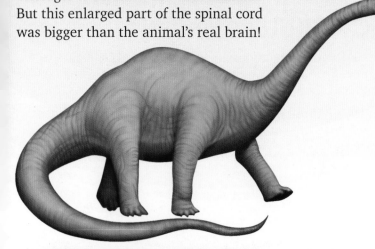

INJURED BRAIN

Because different parts of the brain control different things, a brain can still work even if part of it is damaged or missing. A very unfortunate man named Phineas Gage was badly injured in 1848 while working to build a railroad. An accident with explosives sent a yard-long (.9 m) metal rod all the way through the front part of his skull and brain. In spite of this injury, Phineas Gage survived. However, his personality changed, and after the injury he had a hard time getting along with other people.

SMART BRAIN ||||||||||||||||||||||||||||||||||||||||||||||||||||||||||

You can't compare the intelligence of different animals just by looking at the size of their brains. However, you *can* compare intelligence in different animals of the same species. Scientists studied the sizes of people's brains (from MRI images) and compared them to how well the same people did on IQ tests. They discovered that, on average, smarter people really do have bigger brains.

YOUR REPTILE BRAIN

One theory of how the brain works says that complex brains like humans' evolved by adding onto the less complex brains of the animals from which they're descended. According to that theory, the inner part of your brain is the "reptile brain," responsible for the survival and maintenance of your body. It's like having an alligator in your head!

HALF A BRAIN ||||||||||||||||||||||||||||||||||||||||||||||||||||||

Some birds can sleep using only half of their brain at a time. If a duck is sleeping with only one eye closed, the side of the brain controlling the closed eye is asleep. The side that controls the open eye is awake. Each side of the brain is on the opposite side of the head from the eye it controls. This way, a duck can keep an eye out for predators.

SKULL**DETECTIVES**

Suppose you were digging through the dusty attic of an old museum, and came across the skull of an animal you had never seen before. What could you tell about the animal, just from its skull? Here are a few of the questions you might be able to answer:

WHAT DID IT **EAT?**

The teeth and jaws can tell you a lot. If the skull has pointed, tearing teeth, the animal was probably a meat-eater. If it has flat, grinding teeth, the animal ate plants.

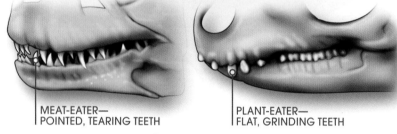

MEAT-EATER—
POINTED, TEARING TEETH

PLANT-EATER—
FLAT, GRINDING TEETH

HOW **STRONG** WERE ITS **JAWS?**

Bones are the framework to which muscles attach. Animals with strong muscles for biting or chewing have big ridges on their skulls where the muscles attached.

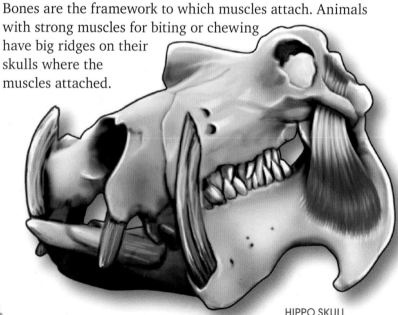

HIPPO SKULL

HOW **DID IT HOLD ITS HEAD?**

The big hole at the base of the skull, called the foramen magnum, is where the spinal cord and nerves go into the brain. The location of this hole shows where the skull meets the spine. In humans the foramen magnum is underneath, because we stand upright.

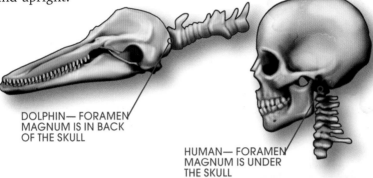

DOLPHIN— FORAMEN MAGNUM IS IN BACK OF THE SKULL

HUMAN— FORAMEN MAGNUM IS UNDER THE SKULL

KNOWING THE BONES ALONE

Paleontologists are the scientists who study fossils. Just about everything they know about the animals they find comes from the fossil bones. Sometimes a skull is all they have to go on! Soft tissues like brains usually don't turn into fossils, but paleontologists have ways of learning about an animal's brain, just from its skull. One way is to make a cast out of plaster or other material, using the inside of the skull's braincase as a mold. The cast gives the scientists an idea of the shape and size of the brain that filled the space when the animal was alive.

READING **BUMPS**

In the 1800s, some people got the idea that a person had certain intelligence, abilities, and even personality, because different parts of that person's brain were bigger or smaller. It was believed that by feeling the shape of the skull, one could tell the shape of the brain underneath. People also thought one could tell how smart a person was, or whether he or she was artistic, moody, or many other things, just from feeling the bumps and curves on the skull! This "science" was called phrenology.

Of course, it turned out not to be true. But these beliefs started some scientists thinking about whether different areas of the brain had different jobs, and that did turn out to be true!

ASSEMBLY**INSTRUCTIONS**

For ease of assembly, the skulls and brains of each animal are grouped together— be careful not to mix them when you open the package.

HUMAN

1. Insert the brain into the left side of the skull.

2. Snap the left and right skull pieces together.

3. Snap the face plate onto the skull.

4. Insert the pins of the jaw into the left and right holes on the skull.

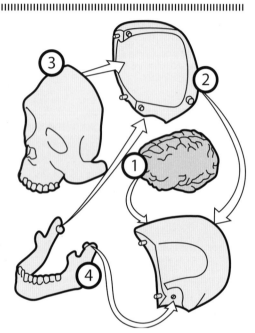

PIRANHA

1. Insert the brain post into the hole on the left side of the skull.

2. Snap the left and right skull pieces together.

3. Insert the pins of the jaw into the left and right holes on the skull.

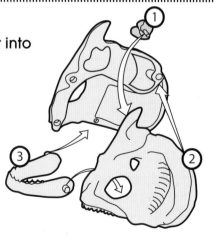

ASSEMBLY INSTRUCTIONS

T. REX ||||||||||||||||||||||||||||||||||||||||||||||||||||||||||||||||||||||||||||||||

1. Snap the left and right skull pieces together. (The brain is glued into place.)

2. Insert the holes of the jaw onto the left and right pins of the skull.

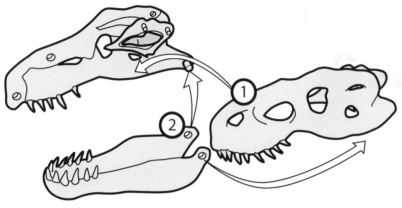

DOLPHIN ||||||||||||||||||||||||||||||||||||||||||||||||||||||||||||||||||||

1. Insert the brain post into the brain post hole.

2. Snap the top and bottom skull halves into place.

3. Insert the pins of the jaw into the left and right holes on the skull.

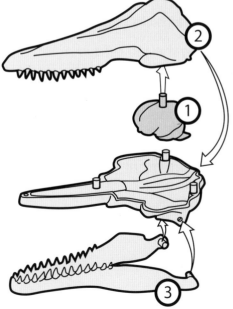

29

ASSEMBLYINSTRUCTIONS

SABERTOOTH ||||||||||||||||||||||||||||||||||||||||||||||||||||||||||||||||||||||

1. Insert the brain post into the brain post hole on the left side of the skull.

2. Snap the left and right skull pieces together.

3. Insert the pins of the jaw into the left and right holes on the skull.

WILD BOAR ||||||||||||||||||||||||||||||||||||||||||||||||||||||||||||||||||||||

1. Insert the brain post into the brain post hole on the left side of the skull.

2. Snap the left and right skull pieces together.

3. Insert the holes of the jaw onto the left and right posts on the skull.

ASSEMBLYINSTRUCTIONS

KOMODO DRAGON ⅏⅏⅏⅏⅏⅏⅏⅏⅏⅏⅏

1. Insert the brain post into the brain post hole on the left side of the skull.

2. Snap the left and right skull pieces together.

3. Insert the holes of the jaw onto the left and right pins of the skull.

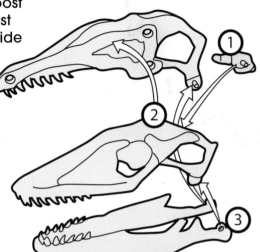

EAGLE ⅏⅏⅏⅏⅏⅏⅏⅏⅏⅏⅏⅏⅏⅏⅏⅏⅏⅏⅏⅏

1. Insert the brain post into the brain post hole on the left side of the skull.

2. Snap the left and right skull pieces together.

3. Insert the pins of the jaw into the left and right holes of the skull.

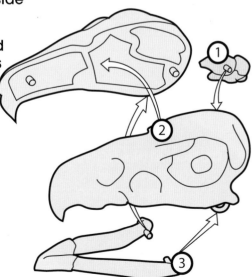

ASSEMBLY**INSTRUCTIONS**

BUILDING YOUR DISPLAY

For ease of assembly, pre-fold the display on the creases.

1. Fold down the left and right sides of the display.

2. Fold the back flaps in.

3. Fold the top flap over the back flaps and under the display.

4. Push the tabs on the top flap into the two holes—locking the display together.

5. Gently press in all of the holes where the skulls will sit.

CONGRATULATIONS!
You have now completed building all your skulls and your display. Insert the skulls in their proper holes and enjoy!

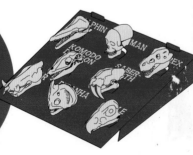